MUD IN OUR MOUTHS

MUD IN OUR MOUTHS

poems

Luiza Flynn-Goodlett

Curbstone Books / Northwestern University Press
Evanston, Illinois

Curbstone Books
Northwestern University Press
www.nupress.northwestern.edu

Copyright © 2025 by Northwestern University. Published 2025 by Curbstone Books / Northwestern University Press. All rights reserved.

Printed in the United States of America

10 9 8 7 6 5 4 3 2 1

Library of Congress Cataloging-in-Publication Data

Names: Flynn–Goodlett, Luiza, author.
Title: Mud in our mouths : poems / Luiza Flynn–Goodlett.
Description: Evanston, Illinois : Curbstone Books/Northwestern University Press, 2025.
Identifiers: LCCN 2024042718 | ISBN 9780810148338 (paperback) | ISBN 9780810148345 (ebook)
Subjects: LCGFT: Poetry.
Classification: LCC PS3606.L9388 M84 2025 | DDC 811/.6—dc23/ eng/20240920
LC record available at https://lccn.loc.gov/2024042718

*For Beverley, Lola, Wicket, and T-Rock,
beloved companions*

TWO

ONE

There's enough order, enough
concrete. The stumps you left

say, *We're all stranded here, won't
get out alive.* So take these shears,

worn at the knuckle, snip under
a node, then place in water until

a life forms. This lay Hippocratic
is all we can offer: yes, *do no harm,*

but also, *some good.* So put down
that chainsaw. The waste of your

lawn has given way to clover—we'll
find a four-leaf if we search together.

I ASK THE GARDEN FOR COMFORT

So she pulls me down

beside the earthworm my

shovel halved, prods until

both sides flex. A few bees

remain to crawl the lupine's

purple throats and emerge

yellow, hawks to cry from

their nest in the oak's heart.

Yes, bougainvillea is more

fuchsia than thorn, nature

brutal, not cruel—watches

us rot, be eaten alive, but

won't recognize borders,

obey laws, work an hour.

Even when long thought

dead, she'll stay secreted

in fungi until our voices

fade and then emerge

to green over footprints.

BEEFSTEAK BEGONIA

To nourish your most
clenched and delicate
parts, you swing about

in a moment that spans
months. Then anything
still in the dark shrivels,

simply falls away, until
your whole clever self
is lit. You may take me,

these soiled rags piled
on my back, for a snail.
Hunched by the weight,

I bow to your bloody
tongues as they open,
one by one, to speak.

THE MOST GLORIOUS BIRDS

Back in Tennessee, starlings, BB-gunned
as pests, rose off fencerows in articulate

curls. Here, gulls quarrel over shreds of
bread. I too once favored the humming,

migratory, endangered. That was before
the rain of mussels, seagulls swooping

to peck at split shells. Before a starling
careened into glass, feathers, up close,

the whole rainbow. Just before we built
this nest from the mud in our mouths.

First, a new barber finds a gap in my hairline

from the fall—not a scar exactly, just my skull

holding its breath. Next, a burner left on—in its

rotten cloud, I peer down the garbage disposal's

throat, then bless summer for windows left open.

Later, almost underfoot, a lobster-sized crawfish

lifts a claw, sidles under rocks. Tonight, Earth

wrecks asteroids on her fontanel. She shatters

time to light and, when her wife runs a thumb

along its milky trail, turns to kiss her wrist.

STAY

Wanting to die isn't the same
as no longer wanting to live—
stepping, for a moment, into
the street. Yes, this isn't even

your worst year, but you're
of an age—horror weighing
pockets like stones. If you
walk down to the river now,

it won't be as before—tears
gumming eyes—but calm
as thumbing a final page
and sliding the book back

onto a shelf. It would mean
you'd seen enough people
who, rather than treat their
pit bull's infection, remove

her eyes; manatees carved
with the president's name;
cities barbed to prevent rest.
Being alive is not the same

as wanting to live, though
drought-stunted magnolias
blush green this morning.
Once, when you were very

young, you camped under
one in a friend's yard, woke
in moonlight and unzipped
the tent to spring's white

offerings. So in your right
pocket, stones; left, flowers.
Sink fists in them both. Stay.

CAREWORN

The fallacy must have been

cultivated during decades

of dorm rooms, apartments

where bricks molted mold,

bare minimum was boxed

to keep—I'm perplexed by

how silver tarnishes, paint

scrubs off ladles, rags get

dingier. What a shock to

inhabit what I'd only sped

past, viewed from a train—

green smears, blue stripe

of river. And hard to trust

what holds still—hangs

frames, fills rooms with

animal smell, breathes

into my hair all night.

GOOD WORK

Nothing can be made
to grow, unwillingly

flower. That much is
beyond us. Prehensile

and hinged at the hips,
we can only bow before

the earth, drag it with
implements to amend

what the worms have
underway, tip watering

cans to assist the clouds.
There are worse things,

certainly. Just July and
fires are already burning

up north, smoke yet to
reach us, so we crouch

in the dirt. Birds above
think we're deer, flashes

of brown in the bushes.
But we're busy being born

backward, digging these
graves to fill with flowers.

THE MURKY SLIPPER

Is where the creek idles,

thick with rot—carefully

shuffle across or end up

soaked and bruised. Of

course, the waterfall is

just after. But that's all

upstream from where

you now pause, jeans

rolled up, to let water

flow between calves

toward further falls or

eddies where crawfish

lift heavy claws—still,

you can't rest long here

in the middle of your life,

such green light streaming

down through the trees.

IN OAKLAND

We got the trashcan fires

promised by '80s dystopian

movies—acrid fumes, and

when we pull blinds, Grand

Avenue's alight. A handful

of protesters, to hold body-

armored cops off, gathered

recycling bins for kindling.

As a loudspeaker demands

dispersal, vehicles advance

and shadows streak toward

the lake. By morning, our

charred cans are back, not

the woman asleep in bed,

man selling loosies, child

in a park, crowd chanting

their names in the dark.

SHADOW BOXER

I drift off with slack fingers but
wake to ache, knuckles gouging
the pillow—in still of night, do

I take up those fights I couldn't
when young, too afraid of what

lurked under a fixed smile? *Am
I winning?* I ask the healer. She
shoos ancestors from her shed

so we're alone, then answers by
drawing a coil of smoke from my

navel. I sob at each tug but sleep
like the dead that night, climbing
the future's slick umbilical rope.

CERTAINTIES

The few that exist (birth, death, taxes)

are easily enumerated, others, thin on

the ground, no sunrise assured. After

your latest biopsy, the doctor declares,

Nothing I can see without a microscope.

Our neighbor pulls weeds, back brace

and all. Your mother's recovered when

paramedics arrive. We call these good

signs, despite the trajectory. Then we,

who didn't know our balance was shaky

until this first shattering, make a choice—

turn legs back to third position or crouch

beside what's broken and hear it sing.

HIGHWAY 1

In the eastern shoulder's
scrub and hunched trees,

a doe noses the air, flicks
ears toward car's rumble.

Headlights swim over two
fawns, frozen beside her.

We all hang there a long
moment—her knee lifted

to bolt and your hands
that still smell of my salt

gripping the wheel—then
round a bend, and this

junker—now, ark—ferries
us into the rest of our lives.

THUNDERSTORMS OVER EL REY COURT,
SANTA FE, NM

I float the shallows of a kidney-shaped

pool—all chlorine and shrieking children—

as electric darkness rolls in, but hesitate

when wet feet slap concrete, once alone,

kick toward deep end. Motorist who rolls

down her window to the whirring saucer,

I'd gladly be undone, heart struck to spark.

TORNADO ALLEY

I was born to a gusty season—
dirt basement muffling wails,
flail upending the candle, tin
roof opened like a can—later,
spent recesses hunched under
a gym mat in the girls' room.
There was even a long wait for
siblings who'd sheltered under
an overpass. I tried to shrink
the funnel in rearview, but it
visits to tear eucalyptus up by
the roots, topple a pollarded
sycamore, our whole building
spilling out to touch it. And
tonight, this weather snakes
the coast—before gutters split,
the California pepper moans
against chimney, and it gasps
back in the language of wind.

PRIVATE PROPERTY

Trespassing into gardens
of fern and poppy, I give

what I do not own. You
stake tomatoes one day;

by the next, they're ripe,
burst between our teeth.

We ripen too, wrinkle,
tilt toward the ground.

I can't even keep you
(dozing in a hammock,

book open in your lap)
like the lucky shell at

the bottom of my pocket.
Yes, I got ahead of myself

from the beginning—see
how dust dances when

the wind kicks up like it
always does at sundown.

The brain mostly obscures:
concerned with continuation,
it washes away contractions

with milk and that newborn-
scalp smell. Even repetitive
howl of weak growth plates—

ankles broken, broken again—
fades to story, an emergency-
room Halloween, doctors in

fangs. Of course, some things
pierce, spillways whirlpooling
the dammed lake, but memory

fragments after—rough hand's
grip, not crushed windpipe or
agony itself. Once swaddled

through the unbearable, we're
abandoned on our doorstep,
another clenched fist to nurse.

NOT THAT AGAIN

From a meager deck,

I draw the same three

cards—red dress, hair

ribbon, muddy saddle

shoes—lay the bloody

offering at your feet

like a cat. Shake your

head, and I turn to cut

flowers, but the stalks

leak what we know as

tears, tempt metaphor.

So forgive, and give me

a new body, set marble

of mind inside. Strike

any match you must.

Parents couldn't have known it wouldn't be nuclear,
or theirs, tubercular. Scythe swept, took others, but
its breeze was only a whisper. Across the continent,
my mother walks her street for the first time since
Tuesday's tornado, only recognizes it by remaining
trees, which, given this sudden light, are in bloom.

FOR THE DYING CHICK OUTSIDE
WHOLE FOODS, ALBUQUERQUE, NM

Today's 125, even hotter in a nest,

the sidewalk you smacked onto at

least 150, so ungodly that the dog

is ferried from car to grass in our

arms. Translucent and studded with

pinprick feathers, you loll up at me,

chirping insistently to be nestled in

a box like a mangy kitten and fed

from an eyedropper. But you won't

survive the leak from your small skull,

so I shade you for a moment before

making my way back to the SUV's

arctic AC, what got us both here.

PASSIVE IDEATION

Nothing selfish (subway,
plane, bomb) or bloody

(gun, car, razors). That's
the trouble, not wanting

to cause any, since it will,
inevitably. Even modest

methods (pills, rope, gas)
cause a scene, screaming.

If only there was a gesture,
like the one for drowning

taught to new swimmers,
we could direct to the air

and be plucked, nothing
in our wake but a breeze.

FORGETTING

I've tended wounds so long—
dabbed salve, closed ragged

mouths with gauze—can't
recognize my face without

exclamations, so pick edges
bloody, but dream of stones

flung across a lake that skip
until lost from sight, wake

so polished by sleep's spinning
that I lift a hand to my cheek.

SIBLINGS

Like most, we had slang, secrets,

a favorite gravestone in the Civil

War cemetery, pack of mutts who

followed everywhere, well house

teeming with cottonmouths, creek

that waterfalled into a swimming

hole, cave underneath for daring

into. Like most, thought ourselves

one whirling being with six arms,

at a sign of boredom, shooed out

to scour thickets for blackberries,

return purpled and sweet. Like all,

were bewilderingly cleaved, but

won't accept it, at night, whisper

come and play to the humid air.

LONG DISTANCE

Every Sunday, you speak as I iron,
fold laundry, wash dishes. Sunk in
suds, your voice rises from the sink,

questioning the racket, but *dishes* is
one of my few answers you accept.
After your mother raised seven, no

dishwasher in sight, you swore to be
different but were glued to linoleum
with three of your own. Still, you'd

like a few grandchildren. I can't get it
straight, can't even write this without
words you sounded out on the porch

as I kicked chubby feet in frustration,
so I lift another glass and scrub until
it rings like a small, dangerous bell.

Yes, the red-tail who swooped across
our windshield didn't *actually* vanish
into the gulley, circles still. And when

the alarm wakes you, I trust that soft
nest of curls will be safely conveyed
to hover at a chalkboard, fall in your

eyes. But the calls keep getting closer.
So straighten your tie, hope we aren't
followed again and someone hears our

voices before seeing you in the ladies'
room. Maybe this is what mom meant
by, *I don't want your life to be harder.*

Driving, you didn't see that the hawk
veered just in time, so wear it lightly—
an asterisk's pronged, golden crown.

FOR QUEEN ANNE'S LACE, CAIRO, IL

Your white wave crests the levee

in this last town before our long

haul down two-lane roads looping

the Bible Belt. We stop for gas on

a cadaverous main street, step into

an overgrown lot to let our dog sniff

your toes. Wild carrot, we too are

thought poison—at attendant's glare,

drive the final leg in one go, but stay

sweet, a pinprick of red at our hearts.

AUTO-RESPONSE RE: PASTORAL

Nature no longer cares
to stand for childhood
or anything else you've

lost and still moon over.
Boiled degree by deadly
degree, it has dying to

attend to and so sends
regrets, isn't available
to serve as metaphor of

fleeting loveliness, can't
supply bees to flit near
a lover's downy cheek,

henceforth, is simply its
beleaguered, brutal self—
worms twisting bones

of your first pet, heron's
steps that flush minnows,
a heavy rain of camellia

blossoms. In a pond far
off your path, its newts
spawn, churning water.

DANGERS

Like the girl we see tackled, roll her
a smoke as she rubs the sore shoulder
where her purse was yanked free; or,

out night-jogging, the man who holds
a bowie knife at his hip and watches

passing women with his whole body;
even the frat boys chucking hatchets
at redwoods beside an intersection

as girlfriends pass a flask. Countless
see the salt circles of others' bodies,

toe them open. Told the creek held
geodes, I went willingly, have tasted
nothing but the salt scattered since.

TWO

We focus on form, breathing at intervals, and try to forget

the water, too proud to admit it scares us—endless, cyclical,

it streams off braids as they swing. But we can't stop it from

going on for fathoms, buoying us like the school of sardines

peppering a wave. If we dove, we'd see a banana-smeared high

chair, dirt shoveled over a casket, great-grandmother's intricate

needlework, sun winking out—future gone, past just ahead.

We cook what your mother craves—

salmon, curry, flan—but she won't

touch it, instead, comes downstairs

with jewelry boxes, hands over all

she'll *never wear again*, which if we

don't want, we're instructed to haul

to Goodwill with the NordicTrack.

The third day, we're hours into *Pride*

and Prejudice when the bird feeder

swings into view, so she tells of last

winter's miracle—on bare trees, she

swears, settled at least thirty robins,

red beads to loop her waiting neck.

GRANDMOTHER'S BODY

To me, buttoned
to the throat, neat

as curio shelves
with a miniature

Eiffel Tower, pins
shaped like sheep,

but it wasn't always
so—photo albums

evidence another
that held to light

like stained glass,
asked daughter-in-

law, *Don't you just
find men repulsive?*

and didn't laugh
because it wasn't

a joke. Cleaning
out the condo, we

unfold that body
from a shoebox—

so silky, she slips
from our hands.

I come from those who sliced branches off
blighted ones, grafted elsewhere. I too carry
shears, worry the handle. My taproot's rotten

on both sides—one's a scrum of drunks; other,
the owners of people, all tallied in documents
donated to the museum. How easy to snip my

last name, a paper doll, from those margins,
shut the cabinet. But when shears slip and
open a flap, that same sap flows, whiskey-red.

I'm made of the damn stuff. See it dribble
out of my mouth, over the vast white page.

IN THE PRODUCE SECTION OF
SUPER WALMART, UNION CITY, TN

No parsley, broccolini, or scallions,

but a plethora of camo—*woodland,*

real tree, mossy oak, the rare *desert*—

so I fill my cart with anything fresh,

head to a checkout where they sell

Marlboro Lights for your mom. And

you wait in the car—between a van

emblazoned with *a country that wages*

war on its police must make peace

with its criminals and a motorcycle

flying the Betsy Ross—as I unload

a wilted garden onto the belt behind

jerky and cartons and, beyond glass

doors, see the child you were—curls

crushed under a cap, slumped down

in the seat. Barely here. Almost gone.

At least, in our apartment.
Outside, maybe not. Seems
men can't stand what won't
come when called, snarl as
pace quickens. Sure, clubs
are no longer raided, red

light urging, *Hurry—switch
partners*. And we *can* make
yearly pilgrimages to towns
that spawned us, avoiding
truck-stop bathrooms along
the way. But it's provisional

grace, mouths *fags* once we
clear the porch. And those
who guilt, *Come home*, never
saw that slip of sand where,
naked except fog, we swim
under a rusty Golden bow.

DOLLIES

I called mine Pussycat, though she was a sack-

bodied baby who, when tilted, batted obscene

lashes with a sigh-like cry. When a girl first took

me home, her bunny's button eyes watched as we

fumbled. We all gripped them, despite ourselves,

in the night. Years later, the stuffed turtle, Silas, is

schlepped cross-country, nestled in a shared bed.

Only after we marry does she give him one final

squeeze, ask me to do the honors. So as I lower

his bulk, pilled from decades of being held, into

the dumpster, I thank him, take the next shift.

FOR A DILDO IN THE GRASS AT
VETERAN'S PARK, UNION CITY, TN

Mistaken for a dog toy at first,

your curl beckons to the pond

studded with snapping turtles

and frog-song at night, where,

at the end of a short pier, it

gets dark enough to whisper

that, even here, is pleasure.

LAST GASP

That's how these years will seem—a breath

above the current, long enough to glimpse

a conifer-lined shore, swim in that direction.

But here, in it, respite is endless as a summer

afternoon, wasps troubling the pitcher of tea,

and having come, dented, through hailstorms,

we settle in. But such fevers break. So I slip

into past tense, hold sweetness in my cheek

like hard candy I can't bear to finish. And

what did you say while kneading dough,

chin flour-white? *Most aren't even given this.*

SCAB

I'm not the only one
who picks it bloody—

lifts rock to worms'
twist. As headstone,

buffed by centuries
of rain, nudges grass

aside, coffin shreds
like blades of grass,

your remains rise—
thumb bone again

thimble-crowned
as dirt falls like rain.

ORPHANS

Both parents

lose mothers

to this hungry

year, so enter

their seventh

decade shorn

of antecedent,

oldest now of

their line, yet,

children again—

quilt pulled to

chin, breathing

in the darkness.

You're again at patio-edge, Virginia Slim lit,
facing pines that block a pasture. Just inside

the screen door, I disassemble a cast-iron toy
kitchen, my knees patterned by carpet. Close

as we ever were, I watch as you shift from one
foot to the other, either humming or crying.

EVIDENCE LOCKER

Mother's downsizing,

hands over a shoebox
of snapshots labeled in

a loopy childish hand.

I stash it in the closet
until bored, still don't

expect my crime-scene-

red dress, menagerie
along the collar. I'm

barefoot at creek-edge,

squinting into the sun.
It hadn't happened yet—

proof's in how my face

opens, wobbly as unset
yolk, to whoever holds

the camera. So shred

or kiss it? No, ball it
up to swallow, make

her part of me again.

Rotted in my stocking. *That's
not a metaphor.* Nails sink into

green fur as I grip it—one half
sunken, other, smooth. *Or is,
for what I was born into, out of.*

My siblings', whole, are torn
to share. *Like fingers locked in*

double-jointed claws. I decline;
they're bitter, rinds so thick
a knife is handed around. *Or*

*bile that rises at the mention of
starter homes.* My sister passes

festive napkins, so I carry my
fruit to the kitchen, surrender
it to the trash can—flawless face

glowing atop wrapping paper
as its true remains in lush decay.

Not mother's (knuckles so swollen
the wedding ring won't come off,

between, blue-veined and thin) but
father's, stubby as cigars. Fingers of

wives bent over embroidery, that,
despite my decade of waitressing,

never worked a day, were instead
hewn by parasitic arts—bar, bench,

earlier, plantation. Not accustomed
to meek folding, they clench to fists,

even in sleep. What to do with two
such cudgels? Reach, grope ahead.

Can't recognize it in grandma's first

night at the lakeside house, July 4th

and her birthday—Queenie's endless

barking dared neighbors' judgment,

so, in wee hours, she asked their vet

to put the dog down. Don't see it in

the week she let seven children tack

up fliers, search the shoreline. I've

only known love's derangement, its

deft unhitching, so mother, pitting

the pile of plums into a glass bowl,

explains, *She was a practical woman.*

She had a very practical sort of love.

OUR PARENTS' DEATH

Spoken of almost without
a tremor, it takes shape as

a cargo-laden ship, smudge
listing on the horizon. Too

soon, we know, it will dock,
freight fill rooms, seawater

overflow pockets. But that's
a ways off. For now, we're

on the pier, feeding quarters
into a viewer, can just make

out a massive hull, tugboats
alongside, before we're sun-

dizzy and step aside to let
the next in line have a try.

CRIME SCENE

Here, in a wood behind

monkey bars, the stream

spreads muddy fingers as

I lift each leaf, peel slugs

off rocks, stroke moss's

wet tendrils, no closer to

unhitching myself from

this scrap of Tennessee,

facts in my fists. So I'll

exhume the past again,

wash her cheeks in tears.

TO THE PAGE

When everything's blown-apart

meat, no telling whether animal

or human, I crawl to your door,

which opens, as always, into

my own throat. So I wait to

be swallowed, but when air

finally rushes in, it turns song.

Oldest, only church, I lay

offerings of teeth and spit

on your white altar. Like

other gods, you're quiet—

blank and absent for ages—

before thundering back

to sound my bones' bells.

Under this white lid,

your shoebox is full

of baby teeth, pencils

chewed down to nubs.

Ash-gritty, damp with

creek-water, you speak

my many secret names.

      Mirror, I come

      to trouble your

      white veil with

      breath. Only

      uncover and

      I step forward,

      open-throated.

            Song-

            keeper,

            tongue

            of my

            mouth,

            I open

            you.

AUBADE FOR EVERY BROKEN THING, UNION CITY, TN

Your mom's been up all night with Marlboros

we bought, and their smoke snakes through her

hidden closet vent to hang above your sleeping

head. At dawn, I tiptoe to the bathroom, and she

flicks the light off. No curtains, so blinds let in

apple trees along the ridge, and, beyond, sloping

pasture that ends in the gully where your dad

burns anything not destined for compost. Don't

wake yet—let me pull the twin sheet over your

curls, keep the world from its spin a moment as

your breath troubles this smallest thunderstorm.

ORCHIDS

Three transplanted stems,
stoic in snow. What potent

mix of hope and ignorance
obscured the moss clinging

to their roots, quite unlike
courtyard's mud? Though

I've done much the same—
brandished best intentions

to shield my mischief. See,
no matter when you read

this, a man has been shot,
holding a thing nothing

like a gun. Of what use are
intentions to him? A better

question is: Who's allowed
to intend, and who's only

an object of intentions? So
notice how I tell it—a story

of mistake, instead of living
things, their deaths. How,

while you listen, whiteness
cloaks everything in itself.

EXTINCT CLOUDS

Never named or taxonomized, only squinted
at as sunset pinks edges—alongside terrestrial,
aquatic, celestial beauty is dragged down our

throats. I once watched a father jerk his son's
arm from its socket, soak his face's miniature
in tears, so know it isn't difference we abhor—

we catch a reflection and back away, wondering
why our steps exhale dust, darkness fastens like
a cloak, climb into graves exclaiming confusion.

OVERWATER

It's my way of killing—
worried heart mists
until leaves fur mold,

watches you sleep to
memorize moles. My
first cactus shriveled

in a basement room,
so I drowned a snake
plant, rotted a dozen

succulents. And now,
despite resolution of
benevolent neglect, I'm

awake to coo at each
scrap of green and, as
you stir, fill the kettle.

We've both been here before—
gripped the rope, wedged flip-

flops into a ledge, descended—
but on this first day together,

we pace the ridge, can't spot
the break in trees that marks

the path. After a sweaty hour,
about to give up, head back to

the city, you say something so
funny, I double over, and just

there is the worn rope knotted
to a stump. So we climb down—

float the river's throat, words
lost to its singing, and begin.

In the room before you know
it, cornucopias overflow, fruit
fully ripe. The lazy flies buzz.

You are already eating, hands
sticky. You joke and everyone
at the long table laughs, lit by

sunrise—that honeyed moment
before day comes—as someone
raps at the door and you turn.

IN SECURITY

Flush with fever, we tug off
boots, unwind scarves, shuck
laptops into bins. Have you

escaped secondary screening?
Never in this city, drawl thick
as you're taken aside. There's

customary confusion over who
ought to perform the pat-down
as I hover beside the same palms

I stood by when they confiscated
a birdcage, sure its headscarfed
owner stashed explosives under

shredded paper. Her finch got
out, of course, battered endless
windows above a people mover.

When our flight boarded, we left
her posed as Saint Francis—nuts
proffered, lips pursed to whistle.

This time, you're the faint flutter.
And I step into her shadow, open
rib cage to an improbable return.

There are no beige-carpeted bathrooms here.

No frozen lasagna from the salvage grocery.

Not a single pill organizer. The Game Show

Network has been canceled. You won't break

the light fixture by opening a closet door too

wide. No one has lived so long under a thumb

that what its nail collects seems feast. Instead,

the apple orchard is crowned with bees. Leave

windows open, and you'll wake to a doe and

her fawn stepping through dew to wrap fruit

in long tongues. To quiet breath and crunch.

CONFESSIONAL

Although grandma made sure I saw the inside
of a church once a year, there's no communion

for the unbaptized and certainly no sliding into
the lacquered booth to whisper through a screen.

But she can't stop me telling now—how I slipped
the cat's bowl through a crack in the door to avoid

shit-caked fur, eyes yellow with death; shoved my
brother down a slide, broke his arm; never held

infant necks right. So cue absolution, my heavy
plait shorn. A shadow shifts behind the screen—

Is that you, redeemer? Or still me, ear cupped
to my own voice, ready for the good word.

GHOST STORY

I met one. Not in a traditional
getup of chains—mine walked
through the walls of a young life
like mist, took all he could carry,

vanished. Scrying led to objects—
an embroidered dress, mud-caked
shoelaces, geode—held so long in
wondering hands that all traces of

him rubbed off. And, since he was
spirited away to some other school,
along with any memories of those
woods, face lit from above, might

be anywhere, anyone a few years
older. Sheltered by this question's
hook, I summon him—shade with
hands of sand, my only lonely twin.

AGAINST THE SEASON

A magnolia purples after November's

downpour. I know the feeling—born

jaundiced, ear-infected, though mom

refused the tubes. With her leaves all

shed, the tree gleams—a girl turned to

stone, livestock, bracingly cold spring

so she can't run. Understanding trails

like a veil as I sprint down the hallway,

cupping a handful of period blood,

having transformed only into myself.

CHOOSING A TRANSITIONAL OBJECT

Snip Hansons from *Teen Beat* while debating
Taylor versus Zac so passionately a curl escapes
its barrette and your best friend tucks it behind

an ear before it catches on lip gloss. Start a fight
so she'll get picked up early, forgetting a lanyard
on the den's yellow shag. Wander past beehives,

quiet for winter, into the pasture where a hayloft
gasps open. Bite nails bloody telling yourself how
stupid she is, the fence posts kicked for emphasis.

Eat slices of bread from the bag. Then, diary
on knee, scribble page after page of *not a lesbian*
before securing the lock, removing its toy key.

THE PROBLEM WITH BEAUTY

At thirteen, entering classrooms
to murmurs of *What's that smell?*

I'd kill for a small measure, so set
out to serve Beauty, carry books

for her lip-glossed handmaidens,
waste years thinking her Truth's

sister, not a look-alike trotted out
for autographs. Yes, Beauty keeps

rotten company and has penchant
for whiteness, strips Grecian busts

to marble. Truth is instead garish,
always climbing out of some well,

shame on her tongue. But they do
meet, rarely, in a clear, wordless

note—so leave me, foolishly in love
with both and straining to hear.

COLUMBARIUM

I can't picture you in this book-
shaped urn labeled in a cursive
you never mastered. It's behind

glass, so even if still present, you
couldn't hear me whisper, *Mara,
your brother's back in rehab*. It just

doesn't seem possible—I'm here,
eating, sleeping, fucking, while
you're nowhere, hit by a drunk

driver the spring of junior year.
*Mara, you bit my lip, didn't pretend
to be practicing*. Though we never

talked about it. So I rest a palm
on the marble where, if we faced
each other, your heart would be.

THE LIPSTICK LOUNGE

One summer, there's an oxygen bar
upstairs, another, skinheads behind
the dumpster. Always, pool tables,
dartboard felt giving way. Karaoke's

Friday, mulleted owner sidling out
from behind the bar, mic in hand.
Light up anywhere; that law hasn't
reached us. But cabs don't stop, so

you'll want to hitch in a stranger's
truck, bum endless smokes. Maybe
you were born here too, beneath
a sticky banquette, took first steps

to a quavering rendition of "Galileo,"
and are still tethered—heart, that
stall with the bum lock, opens at
a nudge, pays for the next round.

TO MY MOTHER'S EX-HUSBAND

You're not the first to spring
a girl from her family home
with an ultimatum, followed
by refusal at the courthouse

to promise *forever*. Before
my father, every man leaves
bruises on her wrists. You're
no exception—the poet who

faults her penmanship, filing,
large-mouthed laugh, declares,
*There's room for one genius in this
family*, while flicking ash onto

the carpet. Now, tell me—her
only daughter with coal-black
hair (like you, like her father)—
once you tracked her down,

hugely pregnant in Asheville,
did you really offer to take
me *off her hands*? And, just
then, did I start kicking?

GENEALOGY

We duck barbed wire, pocket arrowheads, dare

each other into the kudzu-choked shack, dark

as a cave. This close to the Harpeth, our land

must have been a plantation, and it was home

to sharecroppers, if not the enslaved. Witch

House, we call it, and fear it more than graves

spitting-distance off the porch. Descendants

of those upriver who owned people, our fear

is a half-knowing—the toddler who whispers,

Last time, I was your mommy—that it waits

for us to bow under the eaves, step inside.

I trip up the slope behind
the swing set. *I backflip off*
the waterfall. I curl under
a teacher's desk as adults
whisper in the hall. *I burn*
leeches off my shin, laughing.
Mother tosses my dress in
a trash can, but red peeks
out. *Mutts nose the ridgeline.*
I read at recess, move into
town. *Pockets are jammy with*
berries from my secret thicket.
Trees are tongues, fingers.
My woods, a periwinkle in its
shell. In some dreams, he's
a step behind, gripping my
neck. *In others, I whip about,*
and he's a fawn or barn owl
I spooked after stepping on
a nail. Worst is paralysis
as he balloons above. *And*
what of my lost woods? Or
pathless ones I now pace?
When will I crest the hill,
skirt hissing with leaves?

UNTITLED

Tell again how green
can shoulder through

sidewalk cracks, rain
carve Zion Park from

red rock. The tree our
neighbor chainsawed

sprouts leaves straight
from its stump come

spring. The story's not
in the nothing, but how

a bang came, and then
we became. Yes, even

when the water we're
full of is mostly tears

and today's a cell, joy,
being gaseous, gets in.

AT LOVE'S TRUCK STOP, LARAMIE, WY

Above gas pumps, the sky nurses

a cheek purpled by rain as the dirt

road snakes into prairie, and now

a swallow, I graze each fence post,

prong of barbed wire, bless it with

a sharp wing. Matthew, it's spring,

the season farthest from your death

along this road, like any other, yet

here you are, drawing wildflowers

about shoulders like a cape when

my wife, having braved the ladies'

room, emerges unscathed again as

a trucker leans on his horn, turns

onto the freeway, headed home.

ACKNOWLEDGMENTS

The following chapbook press and literary journals kindly gave permission to reprint poems that appear in this book.

Headmistress Press, in *Tender Age* (2020): "Dangers," "Evidence Locker," "Ghost Story," "In Security," "*It's Easier These Days*," "Our Parents' Death"

Barrow Street: "Last Gasp"

The Boiler: "The Most Glorious Birds"

The Common: "Choosing a Transitional Object"

Five Points: "Apocalypse," "Dollies," "Likeness"

Fugue: "In the Produce Section of Super Walmart, Union City, TN," "A Poem in Which the Family Is Not a Tragedy, Union City, TN"

Gertrude: "The Lipstick Lounge"

Glass: A Journal of Poetry: "Overwater"

The Journal: "Beefsteak Begonia," "Careworn," "Perseids Season"

the minnesota review: "Orchids"

New South: "Against the Season," "Columbarium"

Pleiades: Literature in Context: "Confessional," "Family Tree"

Poetry Northwest: "Genealogy"

Prism Review: "The Christmas Orange," "To My Mother's Ex-Husband"

Salamander: "Aubade for Every Broken Thing, Union City, TN"

The Shallow Ends: A Journal of Poetry: "Highway 1"

Southeast Review: "At Love's Truck Stop, Laramie, WY"

Spillway: "Stay"

Third Coast: "Certainties," "Untitled"

TriQuarterly: "Out of the Woods"

Waxwing: "Auto-Response re: Pastoral," "I Ask the Garden for Comfort," "The Murky Slipper," "Private Property," "To My Neighbor as He Downs Trees"

ZYZZYVA: "Object Permanence"

THANK-YOUS

No one writes alone, and thank goodness for that. I am overwhelmed with gratitude when I reflect on all the love and support that has surrounded me as this book came to be: the family and dear friends who celebrated and supported me through every vicissitude of fortune; the wonderful reading series that allowed me to give these poems voice; the journals that shepherded many of these poems into the world for the first time; and the powerful lesbian force that is Headmistress Press, for publishing some of these poems in *Tender Age,* which won the Charlotte Mew Chapbook Contest in 2019. In so many ways, this book is a gift to and from my family—Ana Anderson and our dog, Winnie. I'm deeply indebted to my writing partner and friend, Sophia Starmack, who kindly stewarded many early drafts. I'm thankful to my editor, Marisa Siegel, whose feedback and support gave the book its final form, and the team at Northwestern University Press for their hard work and gentleness with my words. And I'm grateful to the community of Foglifter Press for spurring me, always, to write toward a better, queerer world.